Taking My Mother to the Opera

To my parents, Joyce and Sydney Brown

Taking My Mother to the Opera

Diane Brown

OTAGO UNIVERSITY PRESS

Acknowledgements

With thanks to the Janet Frame Literary Trust, Peter and Dianne Beatson Fellowship, Emma Neale, Rachel Scott, Wensley Willcox, my family and, as always, Philip Temple.

A **Black** And **White** Story

Your parents were so romantic,
my cousin says. Already the cancer
that will kill her is taking her back.

I was thirteen when I saw them
walking home from the beach.
Your father bare-chested, carrying

Paul on his shoulders, your
mother's hand in his. I thought
he's the kind of man I'd like to marry.

Her voice cracks when she laughs,
I couldn't understand why Nana
didn't like your dad. Mine

wasn't good enough either.
Too loud, given to rude jokes
and hugging. Yours had ideas

above his station. The way
he bought your mother a corsage
and took her to the opera.

Growing up, I never was
interested in the details
of their lives before me,

being happy enough
with the simple narrative:
A whirlwind romance, met

and married in six weeks,
Dad said. Neither of them
pretended the past

was a place they would
take us to—if only they
could remember the way.

They couldn't forget it
but they kept it to themselves
while we got on with the moment.

The dusty albums stored
in the lounge record trips
taken in retirement

and could belong to any couple.
But not these unlabelled,
undated old photos

thrown into shoe boxes
and stacked on the floor
in my old room.

Too late to ask permission,
it's up to me to tease out
some sort of narrative

from the missing story,
to add the words
I never thought to ask.

I pick them from the box
one by one like chocolates: black
and white snaps, salty or sweet,

and peer into their tiny faces
as if we've never met
or just been introduced.

Before the war, my tinsmith
dad is striking a pose on a plinth.
During the week he dreams:

boxing, jiu jitsu, poetry,
photography and surfing on a long
board at Mount Maunganui.

Now, clad in woollen togs, he poses
beside his mother who never wears
anything but calf-length dresses,

navy and white spots, and refuses
to venture below the high-tide mark
for fear of getting wet.

On the back of another snap
someone's written, 'Dad
on holiday with the girls again!'

Bare-chested at the beach, he's
lying outstretched in the arms
of four young women. The question

is not who the women are
but who wrote the commentary
on the back. Not my writing,

nor that of my brothers. But this
is the way of family history: for every
disclosure, another mystery.

Sometimes absence in photos
tells more of a story. My mum's
not at the beach with all seven

of her siblings, lined up
at water's edge in their togs,
for a snapshot. Here,

she's alone in a studio
in her velvet dress, blue
possibly, with sunburst

embroidery, wishing
she wasn't. You can tell
from the look on her face.

Yoked to a plough by Methodist
grandparents, and forced to sit
on her hands all Sunday, bred

a silent defiance. *I stayed sane
by swearing to myself*, Mum says.
Words I was never allowed

to utter in her presence.
She's maintained this one-way
conversation all her life, keeping

her own counsel, allowing
no disclosures, either of anger
or of love to husband and children.

War meant getting away
from home to be a farm girl:
driving tractors, digging the soil,

bunking with girls but no such
thing as lesbianism. Next door,
a bedroom full of onions.

*We could never get rid of the smell
but it was better than millinery—six ribbons
and bows for ten pence an hour.*

On days off: outings to the beach,
hanging upside down from trees,
or swinging a baseball bat.

Later at a party wearing
cowboy dress, strumming a guitar
I never knew she could play.

*Growing up on the farm
I was a tomboy,* Mum says,
when I mention my transgender

sister-in-law. *I could have been
one of those.* Realising what she's said,
she takes it back. *No, not really.*

In the *Auckland Star*, a photo: Mum
in dungarees, legs planted in a field
of lettuces, while the man she's yet

to meet is running over hot Egyptian
sand, in cotton shorts and leather
boots, picking up body parts.

*In Egypt, my mate told me
my girlfriend turned into
the town bike,* Dad says.

*Lucky escape, I reckon.
As for your mother, she refused
to sell herself for silk stockings*

or anything else. He's setting
the bar high, I know it:
but I take after him, not her.

I was hiding behind the hedge,
Dad says, *when your mother
walked by with her new beau:*

*a spiv in a panama hat.
I leapt up, said, Going sailing?
or some other silly thing.*

*Your mother laughed
and that was that.
Love at first sight.*

After the war: a shortage of men.
Always a beauty, Mum had choices
but even with all this time to consider

she allows no smile, no twist
of her curls to say she chose the right one.
Your granddad told me your dad

*was an alcoholic, to dissuade me
from marrying him,* Mum says.
Not true. He wanted him to stay

*home with them forever.
Some parents were like that then
and of course he was an only.*

My favourite photo of Mum snapped
at Cheltenham Beach, where
they appear after their registry wedding,

Mum in sensible tweed suit:
bridal dresses too expensive
and hard to come by; anyway

she prefers saggy togs.
Here she is, laughing at Dad,
as if nothing had ever hurt her.

Not the opera, Dad says,
we never went to the opera,
but the flowers sound right.

I've always bought your mother
flowers, why wouldn't I?
Best woman in the world.

Mum, who doesn't believe in poetry
or any other form of declaration, mutters,
Actions not words, behind his back.

Not tuned in to cynicism, Dad refuses
to hear. It doesn't occur to him
his memory might be fading.

There may have been a time
when they attended *Madame Butterfly,*
Mum wearing her good dress,

the green tulle with a flared skirt;
behind her ears, a dab of Evening
in Paris, from the deep blue bottle.

Dad in white shirt and striped tie,
heart soaring. There are no photos
of this so perhaps I am spinning

the parent tale we all want
to read at bedtime—love
uncomplicated and just for you.

Then We Come Along

Accommodation's scarce:
blame returned soldiers
making up for lost time.

At first, a flat in Parnell
where Dad wakes up screaming,
Where's his head? every night.

On the way to work he falls
off a truck, injures his back,
loses his carpenter's job.

Aunt Ruby offers to pay for training
as a doctor, if he'll agree to become
a missionary. Atheist and principled,

Dad refuses. Nor will he see a *trick
cyclist, madder than their patients.
Sometimes he'd take Paul out*

in his pram for the day, Mum says.
*I never knew where they went
or if they'd come back.*

By the time I come along
they've moved up or down
depending on your point of view

to a two-bedroom state house
below the road in Grey Lynn
on the edge of the dump.

While Mum has a baby, a neighbour
takes me to the zoo where a monkey
grabs the bag of peanuts I am holding

and runs away. The baby sister I want
is a brother. I beg Mum to let Clive's
mass of blond curls grow long.

But he is all boy, an escapologist,
according to Mum, hanging out
the upstairs window by his fingertips.

Damp runs down the walls in winter.
I get pneumonia and nearly die.
Clive bashes Paul on the head

with a hammer as they play wars
in preparation for the next one.
Dad gives them both the strap.

I am so shy I don't speak
at school for six months.
I cry for Paul every lunchtime.

The teacher thinks I am slow
until I open my mouth
and read better than anyone else.

❧

After school, Mummy's
not at the *murder house,*
where she told me to wait.

Maybe I dreamed her up,
will have to live alone now
in the darkening woods

like all bad children
but wait, there by the shops
a woman in a red coat,

with pushchair, striding
along the wrong way.
I run towards her.

❧

I can fly, I know I can:
all I have to do is jump
off the back steps, pump

my legs up and down
like dog-paddling
and the world will be mine.

I can fly over the trees
and the roofs of houses
all the way to school

without getting my feet wet.
I can sail over the head
of that mad big girl

with the funny legs
who sometimes blocks my way.
Polio, my mum says.

Mum doesn't know I can fly;
it's a secret between me
and me, the sky is full

of clouds, but no one
is riding them, perhaps
it's forbidden.

So easy in my dreams
but I am not very good
at dog-paddling in water

and the air doesn't keep
promises either, letting me
fall hard onto concrete.

Mum sticks a plaster on my knee.
That might leave a scar, she says,
silly girl, what were you thinking?

Big Talk

Visiting Grandma and Granddad
takes almost a day: bus to the city, ferry
to Devonport, two more buses to the Bays.

Getting up Sheriff's Hill, touch and go,
I hold my breath and push on the back
of the seat; every little bit helps.

When we get there, Granddad
hands out aniseed balls, furry
from his pocket, makes us soda water

from the siphon with the glass jar
and the mesh sleeve in case
it explodes. We keep hoping.

Usually there's shouting. Granddad
and Dad arguing politics. Dad
for Labour, Granddad for National.

Dad in a bad mood all the way home.
*I don't know why you allow
yourself to get so worked up,* Mum says.

*It's bad for your ulcer.
Not so hard to keep your mouth shut.
I've had a lifetime's practice.*

Pop lives across the road
from the racecourse with Mum's
unmarried brothers and sister.

On non-racing days, we're allowed
over. Nothing to do but pick up
tickets that lie on the ground.

Don't bring that rubbish home,
Mum says. *Nothing but broken
dreams and sorrow for women.*

Later, she tells me my Uncle Bill
financed his studies by sifting
among them for winning tickets.

Pop, who likes the races,
has a big lump on his neck.
I'm scared of him and my uncles.

My aunt is so pretty with painted nails.
I long to be her when I grow up.
They have an orchard and a section

for vegetables. Mum takes home
a basket full but we don't visit
as often as Grandma and Granddad's

because it's my family,
Mum says, *and I'm one of eight
but your dad is an only.*

The loquat tree in our back yard
is for sissies, my brothers say, jumping
over the fence into the paddock

which merges with the rubbish dump.
There are terrible smells there
and broken glass but the boys

don't care. They dig for treasure
and spray-paint the rats pink,
purple and orange.

One day I sit on the bank
watching the rats scurry in mud.
I wouldn't want to fall down there,

I say, and Max, whose dog bit my bum,
runs up and pushes me. Over and over
I roll, stopping at the mangroves.

No one runs down to help.
I lie there, crying, my new dress
is torn and muddy, my legs

scratched and bleeding. I climb
back up, my ears ringing
with the mocking laughter of boys.

From then on, I keep to the top
of the loquat tree. Under the shade
of its big wide leaves, a place to hide,

a throne to sit on and crown myself Queen.
Far below soldiers run with sticks and rocks,
make war and big talk against our foe.

Bored, I read the latest *Famous Five*,
wishing I was less like Anne, more
like George, a girl but never a sissy.

Who's talking? Dad asks,
as he bounds into the lounge
and does a forward roll,

then stands up and falls flat
onto outstretched arms. *No one,*
we answer. *Well shut up then,* he says.

One night—a roaring outside;
Dad rushes in to tell us a lion's
escaped from the zoo.

We aren't stupid, we believe
he's blowing into a milk bottle
but the roar is loud. I scream anyway.

Things are looking up. Dad gets a car,
no ordinary car, a red Vee-dub,
German, but that doesn't worry him.

He takes Clive and me up the road
for the *8 O'Clock* paper and our Saturday
treat, a box of Black Knight liquorice.

Back in our street he drives
past our house, reckons he can't see it.
Round and round the block

he drives till Clive laughs
so much he throws up
on the back seat.

Saturdays we go to the pictures
and are photographed ourselves,
standing outside some shop

in Queen Street, all five of us
smiling fit to bust
after the film—forgotten now.

On holidays at the beach,
Dad's framing the action: me chasing
the cameraman with seaweed;

Paul with a slingshot; Clive splashing
in the sea; Mum lying still, head
slightly propped up.

We walk across the new
Harbour Bridge; I'm eight years
old and yet to discover vertigo.

It's a long walk over and back, up
and down; below us the Waitemata,
above us, a huge cloudy sky.

By now I suspect I can't fly,
not really. Just in case, Dad
holds my hand firmly.

Mum wants a house of her own,
a garden without rats,
a single room for me, a carport.

Weekends spent driving around
new subdivisions in the Vee-dub,
admiring the latest in designs;

Mum with pencil and pad
to steal ideas, and in her pocket
scissors for cuttings.

No architects or group builders
for them; Dad will employ
his own bare hands.

At night we pore over plans.
I want a house on wheels
to go wherever we go.

Dad lays the foundations
on a section in Takapuna.
A school across the road,

the lake at the end of it,
the beach five minutes walk.
The future is rosy.

And then a woman, a war widow,
she says, asks Dad if she can buy
the section, foundations and all.

Her mum lives next door.
It would be so helpful.
Dad sells it, just like that.

Didn't even ask me, Mum says,
let alone make a profit.
Your dad is too gullible.

Laying the Foundations Again

We start again out west
where the beach is an hour by car
and there's no lake, but a creek to drown in.

Using a black Formica tile, Dad
carves a sea-horse for the centrepiece
on the bathroom floor.

There's a teapot for the kitchen,
and an iron for the laundry
in case anyone gets confused.

Black pointing the bricks, Dad says,
This house will outlast us—
with its aluminium windows, and cork floors,

never to be stepped on by stiletto heels.
His poem warning of hangings
or beheadings should anyone transgress

the rules is stuck to the glass
back door. This is his castle
and visitors are not to be encouraged.

That doesn't stop us from forming
new gangs; wilder here, surrounded
by bush, vineyards, orchards,

creek and railway line—massive
territory for war games,
and the cemetery up the road

to remind us not to go too far.
There're bad men up there, Mum says,
but the bad men can be closer to home.

One day, we see cops across the road.
George Wilder found sleeping in a back shed,
last seen running into the bush.

Nothing wild about my bedroom,
all girly lilac and silver wallpaper,
bows on three walls, stripes on the other.

There's a built-in dressing table, crystal
knobs and a round mirror with bevelled
edges to encourage femininity.

Four horses on the loose
galloping out of control
at the top of the road. I hide

behind the neighbour's fence.
I told them it was wild here.
No one believed me.

The girl across the road listens
when I tell her I can fly. Making
up a plot without structure, I gather

dead crickets, slugs, moss, rabbit tails
and feathers. *This should work,* I say.
It's not hard to spin stories.

Mum lets me walk down
the road to the grocer's.
She's fussy, smelling the cheese,

inspecting the bacon
for fat—too much and it will
have to be taken back.

She counts the change
checks and rechecks, before
putting it carefully away.

I steal a shilling from her purse.
It falls out of my skirt pocket
into the toilet. Lies there glinting.

I'm not willing to put my hand in.
Mum knows I'm the guilty one.
I can tell by looking at you, she says.

We have a place for a table
but no table. We sit in a row
at the low Formica counter.

Mum has to clear a space
on the stainless steel bench
to prepare dinner: savoury mince,

lamb chops, weekend roasts,
home-made fish and chips,
and always dessert—apple pies,

jelly, treacle tart. I'm promoted
to puddings, when Mum gets
a gardening job, and her own money.

My friend Robyn comes to tea.
We giggle so much water pours
out of my nose and onto my plate.

*I can't believe you didn't
get told off for that,* she says.
I might have got slapped.

After midnight Dad bangs
on the wall, interrupting our feast
of fudge. *Go to sleep, you girls.*

We giggle all over again,
safe in the knowledge
he's nothing but loud words.

At Robyn's house we sit
at a table draped in white,
take napkins out of silver rings

and speak when spoken to.
It's terrifying for me. Her mum
teaches us Brownies' table setting.

I get confused every time,
trying to remember the right place
and how to fold table linen.

I never get my badge.
Doesn't matter, Mum says,
Being nice is what counts.

In the boys' room a large table holds
an entire town: a train skirting
around the blue painted lake,

puffing up over the bridge
and through the tunnel under
the green papier-mâché

mountain, built, as always, by Dad.
The neighbours' kids love to visit
but we prefer cushion fights

in the hall, all doors closed.
So dark, you never know
what's coming at you.

In Standard Four the older kids
call me the teacher's pet.
Mr Mann is my best teacher ever.

He runs his warm hand up my leg
all the way to my pants
when I'm reading at his desk.

You're so pretty, he says,
as I sit on his knee in the library,
I could eat you. On our class trip

by train to Wellington, he stretches
up to my bunk, mouth kisses me
goodnight. But Mum refuses

to let me go to school on Saturday
and help him sort books. I scream
and yell but Mum won't budge.

*I don't like the idea of you
going there alone*, she says.
I sulk until Monday.

Dad calls me Princess or Flower Pot
when he teaches us jiu jitsu
at the hall down the road.

*You girls need to know how
to defend yourselves*, he says.
Christina falls like Dad, flat

to the ground without hurting
herself, but I'm too afraid to let go.
Despite years watching him

at the gym, and recurrent
nightmares of being pursued,
I'm his worst pupil, unable

to stop giggling. After a term
he gives up on all of us, persistence
not his strong point or mine.

꙳

One night I wake
to the heaviness of a man
sitting on my bed.

I open my mouth to scream
but nothing comes out.
The man does not speak

or move. I close my eyes,
feel him watching me.
In the morning, the man

is gone. A dream, perhaps,
only it felt so real, so heavy,
it's still with me.

If Only Dad Wasn't an Only

It's raining when we set off, Mum, Dad,
us three and the camping gear
crammed into the Vee-dub,

heads nearly touching the roof,
bottoms cushioned by sleeping bags.
Stuck behind a sheep truck,

the sheep more pinned in than us,
the fetid smell not helping car
sickness, which I try to hold in.

As it is, Dad's heating up.
*I had enough of camping during
the war to last me a lifetime*

*and why anyone needs more
than a toothbrush, togs
and maybe a book, is beyond me.*

Mum keeps quiet the whole way,
even when Dad threatens to turn
back. We stop pinching each other

and keep very still. On the gravel road
I close my eyes. One more bay
and we'll be there. Maybe the rain

will stop and the tent won't leak,
maybe I'll float on the surface of the sea
and watch the sky without drowning.

Maybe Mum and Dad will lie on the sand,
holding hands like they used to
before we came along.

There's a big boy down the road
in the nutty house who looks at me funny.
He doesn't go to school or work.

None of them there do. They play
in the rusty frames of abandoned cars
on the front section. One day

he follows me up the hill, shouting,
Stop! I want to talk to you.
I walk fast but he catches up outside

our house and clutches my arm.
I pull away and tell Dad. He hurries
down the ladder and runs onto the street,

yelling at the boy's fleeing back,
Stay away from my daughter.
Just as well Dad doesn't chase him.

He knows how to kill a man
in a minute, the very spot
on his neck to press.

We get a rental TV. It's the only way
to get Clive back from the neighbour's.
It occupies the best corner of the lounge.

The mosaic table built by Dad is abandoned
for TV trays in front of the tele news.
Every night Dad's riled up over Vietnam.

I'm with the protesters, 100%.
War's an abomination, the very thought
of it stirring up my duodenal.

Light relief in *Get Smart*,
The Addams Family and *Bonanza*;
and trying to kick Paul, supposedly

in his room studying for UE
but actually hiding under the couch,
eyes agog like the rest of us.

Dad takes me to the birth film;
the only dad there but he's been
taking me to movies for years.

He knows I can't bear the sight
of blood but somehow I see
through my fingers—a knife

cutting open a huge extended
stomach, peeling it apart
like an orange, pulling out

a squirming, bloody mess.
I decide heavy petting
is the way to go.

❦

Dad's given up jiu jitsu for yoga.
Mum's not interested in *standing
on her head,* but I have a passion

for self-improvement and tag along.
He's fifty, I'm fifteen. At home we practise
in the lounge but suddenly

I can't stand the sound of his eating,
his big mouth open and talking.
I have a new idea of the ideal.

And unlike my cousin,
I've never admired my dad
as he walked home from the beach.

The girls in my class call me Minnie,
after Minnie Caldwell on *Coronation Street.*
I'm just like her, they say, coming

in at the end of conversations, asking,
what was that? But none of them
have a boyfriend with a car and a job.

I tell them I'm getting married.
Our form teacher is appalled.
But you're so good at Latin,

she says, *you've got potential.*
I tell her I was embellishing
the truth. It's a habit of mine.

Fred, who is real, thinks marriage
is a good idea. He wants to go
the whole way. *Not yet,* I say.

The police are at the door.
A woman's hacked-up body
has been found by the creek.

I didn't see a thing. Rumour says
she refused an offer of marriage.
Is this what happens if you say no?

We campaign for a phone.
Who's going to ring me? Dad says.
Only-child syndrome, Mum mutters

under her breath. Her sisters
all have phones in their state houses
and would ring her if they could.

One day I'm standing
in the phone booth at the bottom
of the road ringing Fred

when a delivery truck drives off,
its tarpaulin somehow attached
to the phone booth, the glass

shattering around me.
I scream so loud, the truck stops.
Lucky only a few cuts, Dad says.

Falling In and Out

Dad would rather I had no boyfriend
but especially dislikes Fred, whose mother
turns out to be Dad's childhood friend.

When they find out who he is,
Mum says, *You have to stop seeing him.*
Your father disapproves.

They have thirteen children and Dad
is suddenly all for female freedom.
Such excess speaks of male indulgence

and what if son follows father? Dad
leaves the dirty work to Mum,
doesn't say a word to me.

Maybe if Dad offered a bribe,
a phone for ditching Fred, I'd listen:
but he doesn't think of that.

Your father says if you're thinking
of leaving school, you might as well
do it now, rather than halfway

through the year: a waste
of money, Mum says. *Besides,*
the economy's getting worse,

and jobs hard to come by.
With no interest in teaching
or nursing, and planning

on marrying, I settle
for a cadetship in the Post Office;
watching the clock tick

my life away, writing poems
on boredom or love, hiding
them under blotters.

Sometimes I retreat to the toilet,
lie on the floor and fall asleep.
Sometimes my boss sits

beside me, pulling his chair close
so his thigh touches mine.
At the bottom of the steps

the men gather to watch me climb
them in my mini. S*ex queen*, one yells.
No one calls me Minnie.

Saturday night I sneak
out of the house wearing a coat
to cover my pink crocheted slip

of a dress, low neckline and holes in
the midriff. *The beach is the only
place to show flesh*, Mum says.

It isn't so much I want to show off,
although my legs are my best feature
and my tanned skin suits pink.

It's just that I can't see the harm
in revelation. And when Fred sulks—
the bikini I buy is too chaste—

I spend hours hidden in my room
trimming the cups and the pants
till he sees what he likes.

Dad drives me to work.
We moan all the way, competing
over who has the worse job.

I can't win. I get to sit inside
all day. He's outside in wind
and rain, in hot and cold,

lugging planks of wood. Not
what I want for a husband
I decide. Already Fred earns more.

I fall out of love with my bedroom,
our whole house in fact, too small,
too far out west. Paul's left home

for parties and surfing. Clive
spreads himself over the mat
Mum made, watching TV still.

Mum and Dad seem disappointed,
especially with me and my shiny
diamond engagement ring.

Fred and I spend weekends
driving round the Shore,
planning a house on the ridge,

a view of Rangitoto or at least
the sea. Inflation is rife
and we are upwardly mobile.

*Let's build a boat, a concrete yacht
and sail around the world
before we settle,* a friend says.

We buy a bach and construct
a boat shed in the front section. No
bathroom but that's built in a day.

Willows to climb and the beach
with the cat's eye shells where I played
as a child is a stone's throw away.

*What's mine is mine and what's
yours is ours*, Dad says to Mum,
a week before my wedding.

That would be right, I say.
You're so spoilt, Dad yells back,
and throws his cup on the floor.

*Do you realise how much
your bloody wedding is costing?
What we could do with the money?*

You've only got one daughter, I counter.
*Why can't you be happy for me?
We're going places.* The subtext is clear.

Mum retreats, crying, to their bedroom.
Dad roars off in his car. No one
speaks when he returns, hours later.

I know he's thinking I'm too young,
Fred will turn into his father,
force baby after baby on me.

Even so, in the bridal car Dad
doesn't say a word, suggest
we go home or tell me I'm beautiful.

In the church he doesn't believe in
he takes my arm, stiffly walks
the aisle, gives me away without a kiss.

Leaping into the **Twenty-first Century**

In Glen Eden among the $2 dollar shops
Dad stops outside an old-fashioned
hardware store. *Fred owns this shop*, he says.

Let's go in, I say. Fred walks towards
us, embraces me in his long arms.
Last time we met at a friend's party,

twenty odd years ago. His wife, at home,
sick, he said. On my own I talked
too much. He said a few words, left early.

This time, we speak of family, grief and joy.
I am married again. *Third time lucky*, I say.
He pats his—new to me—paunch.

He eats well, travels often: to Greece
next month with his wife, the mother
of his three sons, one daughter.

He is surprised by the list of my books:
thought perhaps my first, in which
he featured, might have been my last.

At twenty, I sat in the willow writing
poems about nothing, while he built
the yacht to take us around the world.

His hair, grey now, matches his eyes.
When I leave, his arm slips around my back
as if by habit. Fourth of July, I realise later.

On this day forty years ago I wore
a white crêpe gown and lace veil.
He wore a white rose in his lapel.

We were young; we were beautiful.
Nothing could go wrong. If it hadn't
I'd be a wealthy woman now,

selling nails to fill in time;
my mind replaying the five years
we might have spent sailing

across oceans. At our clifftop
home, shelves of albums
to show our grandkids.

But you've had an interesting life, Dad says.
I consider the poems that wrote themselves
after Fred's affair; of my life since:

lovers, husbands, sons, and my heart,
still beating, though at the time
I thought it would surely stop.

Too late to go back, remind Fred
of our anniversary, ask where
he's hidden my ruby ring. I'll live

with the long gaze between us,
before I walked out of his life
again, with love still visible.

In Italy during the war, Dad fell in love.
Not with a woman, although—given
the anonymous photos found in his box—

anything's possible. The evidence is slim:
buxom Italian women working
like Mum in fields, smiling, friendly,

but no apparent eyes of love
for the photographer. Also in the box,
small black and white images:

paintings on walls and ceilings,
sculptures everywhere, town
squares, doors, domes and bridges.

*Took your breath away from the cold,
the hunger, and the horror,* Dad says.
We did it to be free; we did it for you.

Lately, his conversation reaches
back to childhood, his job
in the ice-cream shop rolling whoppers.

The details that stick in the mind.
Seven when he sailed here.
Eskimo Pies in Colón as their ship

passed through the Panama Canal
ten years after it opened the way
to the Promised Land.

Instead of meat and pastry, chocolate
and cream turned into ice. Magic.
Never tasted anything like it.

And in Auckland, a dog, Spot, made up
for no brothers or sisters, and parents
who didn't like him to have friends.

*When they told me I'd won free broadband
for a year,* Dad says, *I fell off the chair, hit
my head on the corner of the desk, was out to it.*

*Your mother didn't notice but now
she can't say I'm hogging the phone line.
What's more, it's free, so there's no argument.*

His voice is younger-sounding; his ninetieth
birthday and he can't think of a better present
now he can't drive beyond the shops,

can walk only as far as the cemetery.
Here the world is standing by
in his bedroom. But time's limited,

he can't afford to wait more than a second
for it to flood in. *Really, I've got to stop
talking to you and get online,* he says.

How come I'm the one beating the odds?
he asks, knowing better than anyone
it's nothing to do with what you do. Yoga,

food or good behaviour buy another month
at the most and no defence against the shark
circling the swimmer in the shallows.

On Anzac Day we gather at Paul's, high
above the bush, straight eye-line to Lion Rock.
After lunch, we head to the beach,

listen to the piper's 'Last Post', rising
beyond dogs barking and kids splashing
in the creek. A joyous occasion,

save for the dwindling marchers;
Dad frailer every year but still
standing ram-rod on parade.

After, there'll be no rum at the Piha RSA;
his mourning's tightly curled and private.
His persistent melancholy

an uneasy marriage with family jokes,
but he's chuffed the young have started
attending, asking the questions

we never wanted to ask or feared
to unleash, all of us retaining childhood
memories of innocent dreaming

(flying in a tutu over the sea)
broken apart by dreadful screaming
from the master bedroom.

Back home, as a family man, he struggled
to be easy with workmates who wanted
to talk rugby and racing over smoko,

not art or poetry or anything that might
unleash the demons they carried.
The only way was to keep it locked up.

None of us was allowed the key
but sometimes, in a good mood, Dad
opened the box, showed us

the art he'd fallen for. I watched
the distanced look in his eyes,
recognised this place I could never go to.

*You have no idea what it was like
over there*, Dad says, meaning words
are inadequate, meaning he'll never say,

meaning I should never speak
for him, meaning my imagination
is insufficient.

At daybreak I wake with a night sweat;
*captive to an inconvenient placing
of hormones next to the temperature*

control system, so someone said.
I shift bedrooms, slide between clean
cold sheets, read *Breathing the Water*.

When I need it, a book or a slip of paper
appears in my hand, inscribed by yours:
Levertov says, *messages waiting*

on cellar shelves, in forgotten boxes
until I would listen. Her dead father appears
in a dream, as *a blissful foolish rose,*

letting all his knowledge fall. I think
of Dad, never a gardener, holding on
to thorns he's too stubborn to prune.

Outside, a soft spring rain sprinkles
the paper babies I planted yesterday
for no particular reason, other

than they caught my eye, called out
take us, you need us. Perhaps the name
appealed. I open the window,

breathe in the cool damp air, wonder
if Dad has to die before he visits
with something to tell me.

You Can't Eat Poems

You'd better come home, Dad says.
Mum's taken to her bed, refusing
to get up, like some Victorian lady

save she lacks the servants.
Diane! she yells when I get there.
Thinking it's an emergency, I hurry in.

You should have listened to me,
Mum says, *remember years ago,
in that second-hand store in Ranfurly?*

*I told you to buy those old novels
and adapt them.* She points to the story
in the paper, how virginity pledgers

can't get enough of innocence,
novels revolving around glances,
a brush of hands across the table,

never going as far as a kiss,
definitely no biting of apples.
You could be rich by now.

She's not joking. Maybe she's forgotten
the worst accusation she ever flung at me:
obsessed with sex like your father

but at least he didn't write it.
Smirk if you must, she adds,
but you can't eat poems.

You'd think with all her years
spent digging in the garden, she'd
realise there's more to growing

than simply planting seeds,
hoping for the best. Indeed
she tells me so herself.

What a pity you moved south
and can't grow the things you like,
avocados, peppers, feijoas, tamarillos.

There are words I could say;
my garden grows as it should, now
I've accepted its southern limitations

and realised it's bounteous enough:
cavolo nero, silverbeet, spinach, potatoes,
pumpkin, and parsley for fertility.

But Mum's a practical woman, not
one for metaphor, so I hold my tongue
and dig my poems in for winter.

When I turn up with my latest,
she slides her comment across the table
with a cup of tea. *I've never read any*

*of your books and don't intend to.
I've too high an opinion of you
and I'd rather not have it spoilt.*

*Heart poems are the hardest to write.
And sometimes ...* my poet friend
pauses for the diagnosis,

*like a surgeon with a drink problem
you wield the scalpel recklessly,
forgetting to tie off veins.* Then

blood on the floor, poems near death.
His tone that of a doctor delivering
bad news. He can't name another

with this affliction, this insistence.
I could name a litany: *Plath, Sexton, Olds*—
women thrilled by the sight of red.

And me at twelve, displaying my first
bloodied pads to Mum as if we now
held a secret and could be aligned.

She never flinched till she picked up
my first book, read one page, said,
There's more here than I want to know.

When Mum visits me and Fred,
newly married and proud
of our bohemian decorations,

and discovers my naked self,
tastefully pinned up in black
and white on the living-room wall,

she screams and leaves. *Art,
not porn*, I say, not realising
this is a step too far for her.

Didn't know then that openness
would become my way
of speaking, of being:

nothing to hide, setting
me free but in the background
her voice urging, *cover up*.

Years later Mum confesses
to taking down the hems
of my minis, half an inch at a time.

You never even noticed, she says
brimming with pride over her subterfuge.
Such subtle direction.

After retirement my parents travel: a once
in a lifetime European trip and despite
Dad's hatred of camping, yearly visits

to the outback, chewing the fat around
the fire. *Your father changed for the better,*
Mum says, *when he gave up work.*

*Those were the good years. Looking
up at the Eiffel Tower, thinking—Paris,
we're in Paris, I could hardly believe it!*

So not the opera, but Paris in August
when the shops were shut. *All those lovely
clothes in the shop windows and none of them*

open, Mum said, choosing this version of Paris
to tell me the moment she got back home.
If no rain today, tomorrow for sure.

Flowers and flattery but no diamonds
or celebrations for their sixtieth. *Best day
of my life. Love of my life, even now*

with her memory going, poor thing,
Dad says, though something besides
my own failed loves sees me guarded

when it comes to buying into this
idealised story. *Promise me you won't
put her into one of those homes.*

When I bring up a litany of resentments,
all the things I wanted: ballet lessons,
a dog, a cat, a telephone; and later,

their refusing to visit or babysit my boys,
Mum blames Dad, his determination
to only see his point of view.

*He was always happy enough
to buy you ice-creams,* she says,
because then he could have one too.

Over the years Mum's muttering,
*Should have put my foot down,
should have learnt to drive. Should*

have gone where and when I wanted.
If her friends had been made welcome,
I might have overheard similar stories:

a collective reluctance to push their heroes
returned from battle too far; having
been witness to disturbing cries

in the night, and during the day
sudden flares into uncontrolled rages,
threatening the new beginnings.

All around the country, wives holding
their tongues, soft hands and voices
maintaining a fragile layer of peace.

You look like your mother, people say.
Maybe, I say, *but it's Dad who gave me
love for the interior view, for words*

too, as if the other voice within
insisting on practicalities—woollen
undergarments, vegetables,

your own money in the bank,
and the mantra *you can't eat
poetry*—can all be repudiated.

Love is too Dangerous a Word

These days Mum talks of Yorkshire
pudding in wistful tones, as if some long-
lost love never returned from war.

She'd make it—if she were still able
to measure and whisk, and the recipe
hadn't been ripped from her collection.

Crying, she accuses her carers, as if
from a drawer stuffed with a lifetime's
recipes, they've stolen the only

photograph she had of this fictional
lover. More likely, I took it years ago,
believing it was mine by right. Besides,

under the new diet imposed by Dad
—*the diet police,* Yorkshire pudding's
banned along with cheese and bacon.

Restitution is not possible. I cannot find it;
anyway, I've moved on. *This version's light
as a feather*, Nigel Slater says, downplaying

modern guilt. Mum couldn't make sense
of it since she's surrendered all cooking
and shopping to Dad—spends her days

searching for fragments of her past
written on the backs of envelopes
and dreaming of lost loves: roast beef,

gravy and Yorkshires, steak
and kidney pie, broad beans fresh
from the garden, her missing knife.

TV reveals families sitting on the floor
with takeaways in plastic containers.
Parents who have never cooked a single

meal for their children and no idea how.
Apartment towers with microwaves,
fridges and kettle but no kitchen.

Describe your mother's kitchen
is a well-used writing exercise;
there is always something to say, words

straight from the heart or gut. But what
will these children, knowing nothing
of food cooked just for them, recall?

Nostalgia for the physicality of Mum's kitchen
doesn't feature in my memory. Unchanged
for fifty years, it's difficult for me to cook in.

There are no sharp knives, just my sharp
tongue, which Mum ignores; and familiar smells:
vegetable soup missing the shin of beef

these days—still, when my friend visits,
Mum supports her shaky self at the bench,
using cold hands to produce

light scones and whipped cream
as if she senses my friend has never
known this kind of mother's love,

and possibly an unspoken
rebuke for me who has somehow
failed to be so constant.

When my kids were babies
Mum kept most of her beliefs
on nappies, singlets and bedtimes

to herself. Only once or twice
did she allow a criticism
to escape her lips. *To think*

of all the time I spent pureeing
carrots for you and you give
your baby Vegemite sandwiches!

Always she followed a steady practice:
keeping us away from Dad's moods,
stitching together comic book collections

for sick days; sewing dresses for me
with flared floral skirts and crimson
sashes; baking individual pies for tea,

leaving out disliked vegetables, topping
each with our initials carved in pastry,
to be picked off and saved for last. And

always refusing to visit her particular
childhood hell on us. Swearing on her heart,
not the Bible: we would never be forced

to surrender to any pulpit-delivered view
of goodness. Not that she confided her past.
Only in recent years has it slipped into the air.

We're eating Mum's scones with jam
and cream when Mum starts to talk
to my friend. *As a child I was taken*

from my mother, separated from
my brothers and sisters, given
to my grandmother in the Māori way,

only we weren't Māori. My sisters
were jealous of my clothes, my doll,
which I hated. You can have anything

you like in the toy shop, they said,
when I won a competition for writing,
but when it came to choosing,

Aunt Ruby said the train was for boys.
My father would tell me I could stay
in town with my brothers and sisters

but my grandmother would cry
and I'd have to return to the farm.
Always a tug of war between mother

*and grandmother. Years I spent waiting
by the gate for my father to come for me.*
A stray tear betrays her flat telling.

Was that the doll I broke? I ask,
wanting to disrupt her unbearable
sadness—*flinging it out*

*the window because she wasn't a real
sister? Yes, that one,* Mum says,
giving me the look. *The only toy*

*I had. Those porcelain dolls
are valuable now.* I remember
its eyes, cold and creepy.

You are too nice, my husband says,
meaning after rudeness, my son
doesn't deserve the ice-cream I offer him.

Perhaps they are both irritated
by my voice adopting the cadence
of Mum, always anxious not to inflict

her literal childhood yoke on us.
Telling me much later that as the earth
turned over at her eight-year-old feet

she vowed then and there never
to repeat. Even the story of her harnessing
was a secret till Dad let it out.

Did you love your mother? I ask.
Mum is startled by the question.
She plays with the tablecloth,

as if there are thought police in the house,
ready to interrogate and uncover lies.
It's a simple enough question,

requiring only a yes or no answer
but perhaps, like King Lear, I expect
too much, wanting the DNA of love

to be tattooed on our hearts.
*I cared for her. She was so little
and so hardworking,* Mum says.

Nana was not a huggy person,
my cousin told me. *All the family
was like that, not cold exactly*

but not brimming over with warmth.
Three when Nana died, I can vaguely
visualise hiding behind Mum's skirt

in Nana's kitchen. I possess no
memory of her face, her voice,
her smallness, her lack of hugs.

That's terrible, my friends say
when I tell them Mum has never
said *I love you* to me. Strangely,

I can't get worked up about it,
paint myself as victim. Maybe
it's not so strange; she's a natural

at *show don't tell,* and I've no doubt
love is simply too dangerous
a word for her to speak.

On the Lookout

We've just come back from the doctor,
Dad says. *Your mother's house
has no windows, her clock's missing*

*numbers, and she has no idea
what day it is. Clear evidence
of dementia but you're not to tell her.*

I was twenty on the day, Dad took me
into the bedroom where his dead
mother lay. *You should see a body,*

he said, *so you know.* I saw that
my paralysed Grandma had left
the room—wasn't coming back.

Maybe Mum will die before
she doesn't know who she is, who
I am. I do not tell her banging

her head on the wall will not cure
her faulty memory but this
withholding of information sits uneasily.

Over the phone Mum's voice
has grown thinner, conversation
and curiosity dwindling.

Now it's me dishing out commands:
eat, drink, wash your hands.
Don't slip away.

Grey catches my eye at the edge
of the otherwise green park.
A bird with puffed-out chest

or some kind of treasure?
I go out of my way, find
a silver balloon half-deflated,

its string caught in a bush,
spent, like Mum who every
time I ring sings the same refrain.

Next week, I'll get up,
go out, get my hair cut,
tidy up the back room.

I'm so cold, Mum says in the midst
of an Auckland heatwave. *I need*
to finish my cardigan. It's time.

I bought the wool in Kawerau
when Josh was born. Not hard
to calculate, twenty-seven years

she's been knitting this cardigan,
dark salmon with raglan sleeves.
Maybe it's like writer's block.

One chapter a year, all
you can manage before fear
grips your fingers.

A TED talk woman recommends
taking up repetitive hobbies
while you're young: rag rugs, say,

or crocheting; a matter of training
your hands for when the mind
goes absent. I order the wool.

After a bad dream I remember
it's Mum who's in hospital, mouth
closed against food or water.

Lucky your mother's still around,
friends say, but how much longer
can luck hold? All my life

she has pulled me out of harm's way,
slipped money into my pocket,
recommended the wearing of singlets,

wool preferably, advised the right month
to plant garlic and tomatoes, suggested
next time I marry a man who knows

how to fix things, and who'll accept
me keeping my own counsel,
my own thoughts, my own bank account.

I've not wanted or heeded
her cautionary commands. *Don't
walk alone at night in the bush,*

*or on the rocks where you fell
so badly. Don't go south
where it snows in spring*

*and is too cold for your bones.
Don't reveal your legs, your
chest, your life, your heart.*

There are four beds in Mum's
hospital room. Parked in the one
nearest the door: an old woman,

her head pressed into the pillow,
silvery-grey curls grown limp.
I walk right past her.

*Remember the time I lost you
after school?* I say, circling
back to the bed by the door.

*I was five and thought
I'd never see you again and then
you were there in your red coat.*

I can still see the image, I say.
I never had a red coat,
Mum says.

I'm preparing for the cold
like she taught me, knitting
undergarments of steel

but I'm not yet ready. *Wait.*
Slow like her but I'll get there
—soon. Not far to go.

Fauns left by their mothers
*lie unmoving, camouflaged
and scentless*, says Wallace Stegner

in *Crossing to Safety,* as if
he knows the way Mum sits,
has always sat watching

some old internal movie
with sad music roll on, her face
so passive, so unrevealing.

Listening to My Father Read

One a.m. The phone rings. Not
the usual drunk partygoer wanting
a taxi. *Dad's dying,* Clive says.

I lie in bed trembling on the border
of new territory. In the morning,
work to cancel, a plane to catch.

He's still alive when I get there.
A nurse-aide is on twenty-four-hour care;
he's free of tubes and curled in foetal position.

Not eating or drinking, the nurse says.
I wonder how that would be possible,
with eyes shut tight and writhing in pain.

Dad, I say, and take his hand.
He opens his eyes and bares his teeth
in a terrible grin. A silent scream.

His mouth's open and he's panting
like a thirsty dog. *Want some water?*
He nods. I drip it from my bottle,

down his throat. *Promise me
you'll put a pillow over my head
if I end up in a bad way*, he once said.

I don't think I could, I'd said,
harbouring no illusions. *Then Clive
better have power of attorney*, he said.

The next morning, Dad's sitting up
eating a sandwich. His eyes hook
into mine. He doesn't thank me

for my gift of possible life but I suspect
he would have done the same for me.
Not so long ago, he declared,

You're the light of my life.
I thought that was Mum, I said.
No, she's the love; you're the light.

On my next visit he smiles absently
as if I am his nurse, not his light.
He has invented a new language:

a fast-spoken outpouring of rhyming
sounds, for which there is no dictionary.
Plukey pluke, churges, turges.

He was always fond of chime
and made-up words, fan of Milligan
and Lear and anyone subversive.

He went as far as writing a poem
in response to my dislike of rhyme.
Assonance or dissonance, that is the query

today's answer is far from cheery
seems people prefer discordance
in their poetry to concordance.

Think of Milton minus Stilton
Not to mention Donne long gone
It would not Sitwell with Sacheverell.

Ezra Pound is underground
Geoffrey Chaucer is no more
Richard Lovelace knew his place.

Have a care for de la Mare.
See I cannot cease my rhyming
It's terrible this harmonising.

This cloned impersonator
who is not able to show or tell me
he wants me here or not, has taken

to wandering into other patients'
rooms at night, walking off
with their glasses or false teeth.

Ninety-two, but dying put on hold for now.
After the family conference
I've got to fly back to Dunedin, I say.

Dad laughs, though my move
there so far south
was deemed a betrayal.

We are all in the room with Dad
as the doctor shows us two large
white spots on the scan: bleeding

on opposite sides of his brain.
An unusual occurrence, should
be dead but this is a man

who thought nothing of walking
into the doctor's on a broken hip
a year ago. *Should have died*

then, the GP said. *A stubborn idiot
but my favourite patient, such
an intelligent man, so much to say.*

They're not sure if it's tumour
or stroke but at his age there's no
point to diagnosis or treatment.

Dad sits up, his back straight as ever,
apparently listening, but his eyes
unfocused. *Recovery is unlikely*,

the specialist says. Then someone
I want to slap adds, *You can't
go home, you can never go home.*

Words fired like a bullet. Dad
slumps in his chair. Tears cascade
down his face, without a sound.

He liked to be the bearer of news
maintaining a daily habit—reading
articles aloud to Mum usually,

but sometimes selecting me
to listen over the phone, resisting
all attempts at diversions,

questions asking for his opinion,
or the delivery of mine. Sometimes
adding long accounts of incidents

with call centres or cold callers.
It was a matter of receiving the facts
as reported, summary never his forte.

Now, he picks up a women's magazine
and reads, cadence rising and falling
as before, seemingly making sense

to an alien perhaps, but not to me,
struggling to decipher one
recognisable word in his babble.

Dad, I say, desperate for connection,
I'm driving your car. He raises
his hands, makes a cry of mock alarm

similar to the silly noises he made
when I was a kid and imparting
a tale of disaster: my best hat

blown into the creek and floating
downstream, my Christmas cracker
ring falling down the plug hole.

While the other patients lie still
and silent in the hospital ward,
Dad resumes reading

and laughing to himself as if
he's clutching his last skill.
The car is lost to him as we are.

All he has is this strange language
we cannot translate or ignore,
brought back from wherever he's been.

Dad's New Home

Back home I find myself, like Dad,
on nocturnal wanderings, legs reluctant
to hold me. I reach for the drawers

for support only to find them
missing, along with everything else
I have been relying on:

my grandfather's medicine cabinet
to remind me I come from people
who worked with their hands,

the paintings that denote a move
up the social scale, the photographs
of my younger self naked,

the clothes to conceal my older self,
the makeup and jewellery to distract
from the truth in the mirror.

No mystery in this absence:
everything's stored in the spare room
while we paint the walls a colour

designed for calm. Now
in this bare cell, inhabited
only by the bed and us

I realise there is something
to be said for undressed
walls and no going back.

On my first visit to his new locked home
I find Dad in the TV room, surrounded
by women in various states of absence.

He's happy and not confused to see me,
all arrivals and departures accepted
as a matter of course, as fate.

Do you want to show me your room?
I say, and he stands up. *Take my cup*,
his stringy-haired companion insists.

I decline and follow Dad down
the corridor. With his walker he stands
upright as ever, frail but young looking.

His clothes are reduced to three drawers
with labels: *tops, pants, underwear*.
There's a bed, a hand basin, a wardrobe,

and a rocker with a fraying cover.
The window looks out to the garden.
Sparrows flaunt their freedom.

Dad opens his underwear drawer,
takes out some family photos and tries
to give them to me, along with the pile

of clean clothes sitting on his tray table.
Clearly he wants me to take them away,
as if he's decided to renounce family.

We are all in the Christmas photo taken
a year ago but in the folder that purports
to tell of his life, I am not listed.

Too far away to be of use, no doubt
my brothers think, though they know
I am, or was, his favourite.

*They want to kill me, I am mad, too late
for me, I know I am mad*, he says,
suddenly making sense. Perhaps

nonsensical words are easier to bear,
after all. In the rare times Dad talked
of the war, he mentioned soldiers trying

to be declared insane and sent home.
If they were that desperate, they were
clearly sane, he'd said. Catch 22,

before the term was created. He knows
all about endurance, of course,
and the impotency of complaint.

From his shirt pocket Dad pulls
a small packet and hands it to me
while keeping an eye on the door.

He points to my bag, as if playing
charades. *Don't show*, he says.
When he resumes his non-stop,

non-eye-contact conversation,
I unravel his present. Bits of a broken
cup wrapped in a magazine page,

along with minute pieces of paper,
systematically torn. My instincts
are to reassemble the jigsaw,

decipher the code that might end
incarceration. Nothing is hand-written
on the paper, no words circled.

I'm told he can't write. Perhaps
the message is simple: he needs to conceal
the broken cup from the powers that be.

Only I want something more.
Talking rubbish, I know I am.
Too late for me, he says, *but Mum …*

Mum's all right, I say, *don't worry about her.*
I lie but what's the point in accusations?
Controlling money, medicines, shopping,

all the running of the household,
now he's partially disappeared, Mum
is all at sea, even the remotes a mystery.

I find myself crying. *Don't cry*, he says,
as if he's back with me. Then, *I love you
very much* is threaded into a long string

of non-words, like coming across
New Zealand mentioned in a foreign
newspaper when you're homesick.

He never could bear witness to my tears.
The last time I sobbed in front of Dad,
he swore at me and left the room.

Now softer, he takes my hand and kisses
it but love is not enough to see me
smuggle him out with his broken cup.

He walks me to the outer door. *There's
your car*, I say, pointing outside, taking
liberties I was never allowed before.

Oh, he says and laughs. He stands at the doorway
and watches me leave. By the time I drive off
he has turned away and is walking back

to the barracks as he knows he must.
The car is thirty years old and without
power steering, hard to drive. *Don't sell it,*

Mum says, *it's my exit plan.* She's thinking
of her cousin and his wife, the way
they gassed themselves when it came to this.

Taking Off

Blogging at dawn to myself;
is this solipsism or poetic practice?
Snow settling the first day of winter.

I'm considering buying a *La-Z-Boy*.
It'll last thirty years, the salesman says.
Is that enough? Clive wants

to throw out the extra cushions
on Dad's. *He's not dead yet*, I say
—only I can't ring him, indulge

both our habits of reframing
activities for mutual amusement.
As for his car, it's sold.

The first call tells me, *Dad's escaped.*
They don't know where he is. The next,
he's in hospital, unconscious.

In Italy during the war he went
AWOL twice. *Worth it*, he said,
to see the architecture and art,

his head turned permanently in Florence,
by the *Gates of Paradise* at the Battistero.
Little wonder, then, to discover

he's taken off from the rest home
on a stolen walker dressed in his best—
shoes, shirt, good pants and hat.

In the end, a rush of blood to his head
felled him short. At first I thought
collapsing on the footpath lacked

dignity, but with walking one
of the few skills left to him, I realised
he'd chosen this: to go not in bed,

surrounded by strangers, but hurrying
down the road to home and wife, the other
great and true beauty in his life.

Sunday morning, driving my friend's car
on the way to visit Dad in hospital,
I stop at the pedestrian crossing.

A Chinese man wearing a white
mask and white gloves steps gingerly
onto the road, waving his arms

as if practising tai-chi or warding off
attackers. What sort of man masks his face
on a clear, sunny day in Bayswater?

And what kind of woman
notices such a man when
her father has just died?

After he broke his hip we had a fight,
maybe the fight of our lives. This time
I didn't hold back my punches.

As a young man Dad was a boxer,
though at home, words were his fists.
Vulnerability didn't suit him; he'd lost

his sprightliness and was suffering
with shingles, *the worst pain of my life.*
He expected me to stay with him,

not take off to England with Philip, whose
stepdad had died. A classic triangle, father
or husband, whose need was the greatest?

Accused of selfishness, something in me
snapped, the way it does when there's
an element of truth. *Where were you*

when I needed you? I spat back.
He had no idea of his shortcomings.
I quoted chapter and verse, everything

I had held on to for years
and thought I had forgiven.
It would reflect better on me

if I'd let it go, got out of the ring,
but perhaps I sensed this might be
the final round. It was now or never.

He took the blow and reeled
back but didn't concede defeat
or say sorry. I said, *I love you, Dad,*

but you can't ask me for too much.
He sat at the table, trembling
and whimpering like a small boy

broken. I rubbed his back
and thought of Lear, blindly
wandering on the heath.

We had a barney but the air's clear now,
Dad told my visiting friend.
She's going to England of course.

*I never could force my daughter
to do anything she didn't want to.*
Reconciliation but low key.

He'd said his piece, I'd said mine,
and could go on my way. *You're
too much alike,* my mother said.

At his funeral, my nephew reads a poem
of Dad's about a computer mouse.
My brothers talk of his liberal ideas,

his practicality, the fridge he built
from car parts, his sense of humour.
A woman who knew him at fourteen,

in the jiu jitsu club, speaks mostly
about herself. She's never going
to stop, I think, but then it's my turn.

I am the speechmaker in the family.
I have Dad's permission, I tell them.
Thinking ahead, he'd paid in advance,

allowing fifty mourners for sandwiches
and cakes; telling the funeral director,
my daughter will do all the talking.

I read a poem of his and then of mine.
None of Dad's army mates are there:
they're all dead. The gatherers

are from Mum's family, friends
of mine and my brothers, my two
ex-husbands and current. My younger

son's in Scotland; he didn't know
what to say when I told him. My older
son doesn't remove sunglasses

or get up to speak. He's been
to funerals of friends but needs,
like Mum, to sit still and mute.

He told me he'd had an unfulfilled life.
He could have done so much more
if not for the war, and the harm

it did him, I say, and add, *he was not*
always an easy man to live with.
Before his stroke I'd told him I would tell

it like he was, but I find myself modifying
and softening—not lying, but omitting.
After all, I do not possess the only truth.

I don't cry, he wouldn't want that,
not when he couldn't solve my pain.
In any case, no one wanted him

to remain in the rest home without
the rug where he practised yoga
and forward rolls; without Mum

and without words. So I laugh, tell jokes,
a performance so polished, I'm watching
myself in the wings, knowing

I'll be embarrassed later, but hoping
he sees I'm trying to do him proud,
hoping he knows what he's given me.

Who Are You?

Back then, my lover and I were
escaping our respective children
to Port Albert, where, I believed,

my great-grandmother came
ashore with the free thinkers.
Places carry memory, my lover said.

The hills, cultivated and grazed
by cows, ran down to the harbour.
Green, and calm, it was saying nothing.

My mother told me her grandmother
was eighteen when she left England. *Running
away,* Mum said, *we don't know why.*

The ship's log recorded Mary Poate, twenty-six.
Twenty-nine, according to her birth certificate.
Eleven years is a long time in a young

woman's life. Enough to get married
and have babies, or not. *Took
her secrets to her grave*, Mum said.

I looked at the man I imagined I loved.
The shape of his nose was just like Dad's.
That must have accounted for it.

I searched the ground for evidence
of Mary's footprints embedded in the sand
as if I would recognise them.

Let's go, my lover said, and kissed me,
the tip of his tongue touching mine.
I was still waiting for the ghost

of my great-grandmother to walk by.
I could say I felt her presence in the air,
could elaborate, exaggerate, as poets do

but I'm not good at lies or poker.
It was starting to rain. We ran to the car.
I turned back for one last look.

No one was waving. A man in a dinghy
rowed past, oars lifting and falling
into water, whispering an ancient lullaby.

In Berlin, then Frankfurt,
in the space of a week, questions
from Māori: am I one of them?

They're going on my eyes,
my colouring, perhaps
my round face and loud laugh.

The more I think about it,
the more I weave a kete
and pack it with supposition.

No one ever told Mum why
she was banished at four,
to the small farm in Cambridge

to paternal grandparents and spinster
aunt. Her older brothers were keen
and would be useful farmhands

but no, only Mum would do.
Because of my hair, Mum said,
my grandmother loved it.

A shock of dark brown curls
surrounded her face, turning
into an Afro if left untamed

and very different to her sisters,
all three pale skinned, straight-haired
blondes with a touch of ginger.

*Grandma loved nothing more than
to imprison me on her lap,
detangle my hair till I screamed.*

Maybe, I surmise, Aunt Ruby,
self-appointed missionary to Māori,
was really Mum's mother—and Mum

therefore, the result of an unsuitable liaison,
or possibly rape, with all evidence wiped
from the records and family memory.

Too much imagination, my cousins say.
But how do you know your mother
was your mother? I ask Mum.

She doesn't even blink.
The boys down the road used
to say, you haven't got

a mother and father, Ruby's
your mother. I never believed them,
kids say these things.

And my mother cried every time
I left after the holidays, but then
my grandmother cried harder

at any suggestion I might not return.
I always gave in, still do—it's
the way I was raised. To please.

Case closed as far as my mother
goes. I can swab her cheek,
have her tested for traces

of another, for whether
her history was a lie,
but do I want this?

To give up the grandmother
with the beautiful flowery hat
and long curls when she was young?

Give up the mother of eight,
who slipped Mum money when Dad
was out of work, who put the Sunday

roast dinner in the oven
before she lay down and died?
Give up her and my aunts, uncles

and cousins, for the spinster
great-aunt dressed in black, with Bible
in hand, supposedly loved by Tainui,

but not by us who suffered the sharp
edges of her tongue, who had called
me a spoilt malingerer, who made

me gag on cold porridge,
and whose long, oiled hair left
a bitter smell in my room?

Out of the blue Mum says, *At Aunt Ruby's
funeral, one of the Kelly boys said
he'd always loved me and still did.*

*His wife, beside him when he told me,
didn't look happy. He was Catholic,
so my father greeted him with a shotgun.*

Forty-five years Aunt Ruby's been dead.
The first time I've heard this story.
What else have I missed?

Hanging Around for Nothing

When I phone Mum, intonation
is no longer enough. I introduce
myself and she speaks at length,

repeating the same phrases over
and over, when all I intend
is to check she's still breathing.

I think I know who I am, what
I have to do today and tomorrow,
but then I discover I am living ahead

of myself, turning up for meetings
a week early as if I'm trying
to speed up time, get it over with.

*I don't like to interfere, you're
always busy*, Mum said years ago,
explaining why she never rang me.

But is it indifference, as some claim,
or a lack of belief in her own space,
her own voice? Inevitably it's harder

and harder for me to ring and face
the circular conversations, the litany
of missing items and food.

Five years since Dad said the dementia word,
Mum's ninety-one and living at home alone,
burning the bottoms clean out of pots.

None left for you to inherit, she says.
Today her slow oven's taking too long
to cook corned beef. There's a summer

storm; they've turned the power
down, reduced its potency, she reckons,
but only in Henderson, mind.

Everything is political or conspiracy.
In Remuera, their ovens burn hot as ever,
she claims. *A different story here.*

I change the subject, tell Mum about
our holiday north, that Philip says
the bad weather follows us wherever we go.

*Follows him, not you, don't you take
the blame*, Mum says, not missing a beat.
Makes me wonder if she was pretending

all along, deliberately omitting windows
and numbers in the dementia test.
Dottiness being one way of escape.

In Auckland, we're taking Mum
to visit her one remaining sister.
It took some persuasion. These days

she doesn't like leaving home,
perhaps afraid she'll never return.
Shall we go past our old house

in Regina Street? I ask. I'd like to show
Philip the first ten years of my life,
though most of the state houses

have been bought by the upwardly
mobile, the rubbish dump filled in
and grassed over, the creek cleaned up.

Absolutely not, Mum says, her voice
vigorous for a moment. *I hated
that house below the road, the way*

*water ran down the walls. I blame
it for your sickness. Myself too,
for not getting you out sooner.*

Since gardening's become too much,
sitting still's a full-time occupation,
her mind coming and going,

knitting a few rows when the mood
takes her, declaring tomorrow
she'll get around to sorting out

the back bedroom, once mine,
now repository for a life: wool, fabrics,
patterns, photos, overflowing bags

of all Dad's belongings. *Simon
would like these, they're hand-made,
he always liked the best*, she says,

handing me shoes. *Too small for Simon*,
I say, but two minutes later she's
trying again to put them in my bag.

Give them to one of your carers,
I say, but she's reluctant, family
being the only charity she'll consider.

Mum's lost her purse, *all my cards in it*.
Her voice quavers down the line.
I might have left it in the hospital.

They've let her return home
but on notice. I tell Mum she has
no cards. *How will I buy food?*

I remind her she doesn't shop any more.
When Dad was incarcerated, it was up
to my brothers and their wives

who as kids never went to the grocer's
for her and don't know her tastes
but are faithful enough.

The food goes into her fridge and since
she's gone off eating gets thrown out
sooner or later. Her younger self

would be horrified at the waste.
As I say goodbye, she cries again.
I've lost my purse. I've nothing for dinner.

She's lucky, I think, knowing that whether
she eats or not, her children continue
to turn up, carrying milk and bread.

Not a lot in common, Mum and I,
apart from the domestic, and even
there we differ in approach. She prefers

the garden to the kitchen, the news
to novels. A sense of humour perhaps,
though more accurate to say

I'm sometimes amused by her sharp
tongue when she dares to unleash it. I have
no memories of her laughing hysterically.

She's always kept her emotions
to herself, private, the way
she was brought up. Sundays

a day for silence and reproach,
save for when they came home
from church in the dark, Mum

forced to lie on the front mudguard
of her granddad's motorbike, her role
to shine the torch into the ditch,

keeping her fear to herself
but allowing her mind to roam unruly
as her famous shock of curls.

Explains why she took up tramping
as a young woman, preferring all her adult
life to be outside; why we were never

christened or sent to Sunday school,
were determined a childhood
free from scripture and rules.

Lately she's beginning to question
herself. *I'm not coming back*, she says.
I wish I believed otherwise, wish

I'd sent you to church so you believed.
Wouldn't have worked, I say, knowing
that along with DNA, we share at least

a realist approach, she finding
her way and peace digging up
the garden, I finding mine in words,

plain-speaking over abstract and no
inclination to believe she'll be waiting
for me, somewhere beyond the clouds.

Now her back's too sore for
gardening, she's sitting at home,
no ticket, no passport,

no bags packed, taking only
what she came with, hair
still thick and curly, eyes

clouding over, ears no longer sharp,
skin newly thin and fragile,
inclined to tear at a touch.

Mind faltering over details—
where she is, what I just said—
but fully alert to her future.

I just wish it would get a move on,
she says. *All this hanging around
for nothing is boring.*

Messages on the Answer Phone and in Magazines

In the air everywhere a constant current
of messages dropped into devices:
phones, computers, waiting

for someone to pick up, respond.
The light's flashing
on my answer phone. *Hello,*

it's your friend. Father died
this morning at Little Sisters of the Poor,
I thought you'd like to know

a stranger's voice insists.
I would but she's not my friend.
My father died two years ago.

There's just my mother left
and my heart set racing when the phone
rings in the dark of night.

So many words, so many demands
when all we want is the warmth
of someone we know,

their presence in the room,
hands offering consolation
when the real call comes.

Mum doesn't have an answer phone,
why would she when she never goes out?
Some days the phone rings and rings

and is not answered. I imagine
the urgency of it, loudest in the kitchen,
where the phone sits on a cake tin,

so it reverberates and echoes down
the dark hallway, famous location
for pillow fights; then into their bedroom,

the tone becoming insistent now;
back up to the lounge where Mum's
knitting sits, one sleeve to go,

the puce colour too insipid for me
to bother finishing it off, and Mum,
lying on the floor, helpless.

The next day, she claims
the phone never rang once.
It'll all be over soon, she says.

I'm not sure if she's reassuring
herself or me. Not sure if there's
a better way to end. Not sure

I'll be able to do her proud.
Just dig a hole for me in the garden,
she says, *and plant a tree on top.*

The call when it comes is not final.
Mum, found on the floor, bruised
but breathing with no bones broken.

Don't know what I'm doing here,
she says, when I visit. *It's so boring
and the woman next to me*

hasn't said a word. The silent
neighbour lies stiff and pale
beneath the thin covers.

Want anything else? the nurse asks Mum,
who yells out, *you could bring
in some more interesting patients.*

*Don't go into hospital, you'll never
go home,* the saying goes and so
it's proven, the judgement given.

She failed the make-a-cup-of-tea-
and-toast trial. *You can no
longer look after yourself.*

The rest home generic like Dad's.
A bed, drawers, wardrobe
but no labels or locks.

I find Mum lying on her bed.
*We're not supposed to lie down
during the day*, she says, *but*

what else is there to do? I Blu-Tack
family photos on the walls
while she takes no notice.

In the dining room
Mum sits at a table with one man
and two women. Everyone

looks at me as I hover beside her
like some monstrous animal
too cheerful and loud.

See that woman over there?
Mum says, pointing to the far corner.
That's Gordon's mother.

Who's Gordon? I ask.
*You must have been in London
when he was around*, Mum says,

and I realise she's talking about
some past boyfriend and has
confused me with my aunt.

How do you know that's his mother?
She always had a funny leg,
Mum says, *and still has.*

She must be at least a hundred and twenty-five,
I say. *He was younger than me*, Mum says.
It's his mother, she knows who I am.

But do we know who she is,
I wonder, when my aunt tells me
Gordon was Mum's fiancé

before Dad, rejected in the end
for being a little wet, a little
boring with his shop job.

Years nagging her to sort
the house out, years the same
answer, *tomorrow*.

Simply procrastination or
something passive-aggressive
in this refusal to face it?

Doesn't she realise I'll make use
of my clearing work, a cool eye
cataloguing her mess, her archaeology?

Under the bathroom basin a leak,
everything rusty or sodden.
It's easier to biff the lot, forty years

of ointments, pills and potions
that did the job or not. Temperature
wands once placed in my mouth,

plasters and bandages, all of it
expecting accidents or illnesses.
None preventing strokes or dementia.

Stripping the bed, under the sheets
I find a notebook with blue plastic cover,
spiral bound. I'm hoping for last words

or answers to long-held secrets
but there are just lists, nearly all involving
bread and milk. But here's a fifty dollar note

secreted into the back pages. *Always
keep some emergency money,
enough for taxi or ambulance*, she'd said.

On the kitchen bench a note, written by Mum.
*MISSING! Poor Johnny's plates brought
back from the Korean War, gold*

and white, MY INHERITANCE.
Found in the bottom
of a laundry basket, Johnny's plates

wrapped in an old tea towel.
Missing: explanations, why
my mother and not Johnny's wife

had the plates in the first place.
Why I never heard the story of poor
Uncle Johnny and his war.

Mum was not one for wasting
time or money on fripperies apart
from a frowned-upon habit

of magazines, piled on her side of the bed.
In my teens I fell upon them, hoping
mysteries would be revealed. How

to apply eyeliner and lipstick and let's
not forget how to greet a man home
from work; all of which my mother deemed

unworthy. Reading, she seemed at a loss,
idly ripping out the odd recipe to be stuffed
in a drawer, never looked at again.

In school holidays, my self-appointed job
was to cull them, keeping those promising
a life beyond motherhood.

I desired a cliché: travel, glamour;
looked up to my childless aunt
with her perfumed skin

and Vogue pattern clothes.
A mystery then as to why I found
it necessary to marry so young.

Now the magazines beside the bed
are glossier, the women airbrushed
and thinner, the articles focused

on having it all. Hoping Mum hasn't
reverted to hiding money between
the pages, I biff them unread into the bin.

To deal with Dad, we have to turn
the plastic urn, lurking under Clive's bed
for the past four years, upside down,

put a coin or a knife in the slot
like breaking into a piggy bank
that may or may not contain treasure,

may or may not contain Dad.
I leave spooning the ashes to Philip:
I don't want Dad sticking to my fingers.

Some we bury in the garden
of the house he was so proud of,
The straightest pointing, even

though I'm a carpenter, not a brickie.
The garden was Mum's domain
but I don't think he'll object.

Fine words do not pass my lips;
my tone is casual, almost flip,
but the very act of talking to him

as if he could hear, and me straining
to pick up some sort of sound or sign,
lends a gravitas Dad would laugh at.

Believe me, I've seen enough death
to know once you're gone, you're gone,
he would say, *that's it. Don't imagine*

I'll be looking down on you.
I am my father's daughter
but the silence is disturbing.

Walking out of the house
carrying a basket full of bottles,
I trip over the back step, land

face down on the concrete.
The Christmas present of boutique
extra virgin olive oil spreads

over the ground, an offering
perhaps to the new residents. I pick
myself up, my face bloody, and later

bruised. Dad's voice in my head,
*Relax your arms, give yourself up
to the fall*—heard too late.

Back home I find my own collection
of shiny covers obscuring the latest
unread novels quietly offering all

I need to know, without shouting.
But there's no escaping inheritance,
the lack of belief in your own wisdom.

The **Final Clearing Out**

On my next visit, the named boxes
I'd left behind sit on the floor.
The milk I bought, long gone bad,

remains in the fridge, but other things
are missing. Nothing valuable,
just the stack of poor Johnny's plates

and Mum's craft bag, filled with wool
I was planning to crochet a rug with,
to keep myself warm over winter,

now Mum has relinquished
her mothering role, ceased
talking about singlets and kidneys.

The TV, reincarnated ten times,
hasn't worked properly since the aerial
blew down in a storm. With Dad not around

to fix it, Mum took to watching the one
in her bedroom. Only now and then, mind,
not being a woman for drama of any kind.

Not much else to see in the lounge:
the pictures on the wall now removed
have left bright rectangular patches

on the green paisley wallpaper.
I'd like to pull down the torn and mouldy
net curtains which once protected

me from the gaze of passing boys,
but settle for removing slip covers
off couches and the heavy brocade cloth

always obscuring the kauri table,
as if stroking its unmarked grain
might ruin it for life.

Under the sheets in the divan drawer
I find a corset, whale-boned, white rose
embossed satin, too small to ever

have fitted me—maybe Mum's?
In the rest home she claims
to have never seen it in her life.

Just junk, my brothers say.
We don't want it either, Philip says.
I carry on filling my boxes

with stained china, silver cutlery,
books, and yellowy white tablecloths.
There are lists everywhere: shopping,

phone numbers, gardening plans,
one with the amount of money
required for a new roof, teeth and death,

but no new poems or love letters
from Dad, none of my childhood
writing, no opera programmes.

❦

Among empty envelopes a photo
of Mum, in bed with my two boys
in their pyjamas, the oldest grinning

or grimacing, it's hard to tell,
the younger clutching a book. Mum,
a few years older than I am now,

dark hair still and smiling. All so
cosy and cuddly I want to wriggle
my way in and stay there forever.

❦

Once visiting I woke to hear Dad
reading the paper to Mum.
I went in and sat on the end

of their bed, drinking a cup
of tea while Dad's words settled
into me, almost a lullaby.

While I grew up with uncertainty
of what and who created the ocean,
the mountains, the sun, the moon

and stars, there was certainty here
in this house, the tea in the morning
and the paper to be disseminated.

❦

Mum tells me she needs shoes,
new summer clothes, pyjamas
and undies. I've stuffed her closet

full and put winter clothes under
her bed but it's not enough,
will never be enough.

Over and over, I've explained
the house is sold as she wanted,
to my nephew, based overseas.

For the moment she understands
she can't grasp why he's not living in it,
then she forgets again.

Every conversation is a lament.
She needs to get home before invaders
break in and steal all her hidden treasures.

*There's stuff taped to the bottom
of the drawers,* she says. She'd walk,
only she's not sure of the way.

I'd take her myself to say goodbye
but know she couldn't bear to see
how we've stripped the place bare.

I won't be back, I declared this morning
to the mover, who's young and has no idea
of a lifetime, but here I am again,

letting myself into the almost empty
house like Goldilocks, lying down
on Mum and Dad's unclothed bed

clutching my head, willing Mum
to appear with a wet cloth
and lemonade to settle my stomach.

Forty years I've been visiting here,
my memories too fresh to indulge
in sepia recall, but just for a minute

I give in to Sunday mornings
burrowing under itchy blankets
to be tickled; picking plums

and mandarins down the back; Christmas
photos of us squinting against the light; sunsets
as easy as looking out of my window.

I leave the house empty-handed,
drive to Piha, feeling like a child again,
always the one suffering car sickness,

Dad stopping just in time. This time
at the top of the hill I stop myself
before throwing up into an ice-cream

container. Lion Rock stands dark
against the sky; the sun has fallen
into the sea. I drive on.

Paul opens the door, avoids
hugging on account of my bug,
says, *you missed the green flash.*

In the middle of the night
I wake thinking of the house
to be rented out to strangers

and unavailable to visit.
Am I turning into my mother,
fretting for what is lost?

Rain is beating hard against
the window, a branch slaps
the deck. A siren wails.

Flowers in the Current

No sign of the drought
gripping the country
on our drive to Titirangi.

Look at all the trees, Mum says,
*so green. We should have
built here, but oh no*

*men think they know best
but they don't.* Still alive
to the possibilities of nuance

then, but blind and deaf
to the crowing rooster
patrolling the carpark,

and when I hand her a small
vanilla ice-cream she stares
like she's forgotten it's for eating.

*On my fourteenth birthday,
I wanted an ice-cream more
than anything,* she says,

but I wasn't allowed one.
Eighty years on, she's got one
and it's dripping down her hand.

At the fruit stall I leave her
in the car. *I'd better get out—
I don't think I've got any veges*,

she says when I get back in.
*I don't know what's happened
to the tomatoes this year.*

You don't need veges, I say.
Why not? she asks. I hesitate
before answering. *They'll have*

your dinner waiting at the home.
Mum picks up the newspaper,
hits her forehead six times with it

and turns to me. *That didn't make
any difference*, she says,
with no trace of irony.

A moment later, she adds,
*I'm thinking it might be time
to move to a rest home.*

I laugh a little. *Wait*, she says
and gives me the kind of look
she used when I was young

and hiding something;
an omniscient stare.
I'm already in one, aren't I?

Back in the home Mum's listening
to an evangelist singing
'The Old Rugged Cross'.

I remember this, she says.
*Deaf Aunt Ruby still singing
after the music had finished*,

*me pulling at her skirt
to get her to stop
I was so embarrassed.*

In my head, *You haven't
got a mother and father,
Ruby's your mother.*

I'm thirteen; see Great Aunt Ruby
all in black and smelling ripe
sitting in the bus I catch

after school. I avert my glance.
Is that you, Diane? she yells.
The other kids smirk.

*What a lovely mother
you have*, the singer says.
And aren't you lucky

*with your lovely daughter
visiting*, he adds, as if
I'm not standing up to leave.

But Mum's gone again,
into the past where I never was,
making it easier to walk away

113

with no memory of her
embarrassing me apart
from our home-sewn tents.

A deliberate choice maybe,
to be quietly spoken, softly sung,
along with rejecting faith

in favour of quiet Sundays
at home and buying us
ice-creams for no good reason.

But she's making up
for all that reticence now,
yelling as I walk away,

Who are all these people
and why am I paying
for them to live with me?

All those discussions we had
in the past when I wanted
her to assert herself,

be independent, learn to drive,
go where you want. Only
now, she's speaking up.

Months later, in Ripon, Yorkshire,
under the arched brick bridge,
we gather a few wild flowers,

look around to check we are alone,
take out the tarnished silver pot
carried all the way from home

and scatter the contents
into the River Skell beside
the lane where Dad was born,

almost a hundred years ago.
I want to call him back,
have him describe changes

in the town and tell me
all the things I never thought
to ask. But too late,

he's swimming downstream
with flowers in the current,
and not looking back.

Published by Otago University Press
Level 1, 398 Cumberland Street
Dunedin, New Zealand
university.press@otago.ac.nz
www.otago.ac.nz/press

First published 2015
Copyright © Diane Brown

The moral rights of the author have been asserted.
ISBN 978-1-927322-15-4

A catalogue record for this book is available from the National Library of New Zealand. This book is copyright. Except for the purpose of fair review, no part may be stored or transmitted in any form or by any means, electronic or mechanical, including recording or storage in any information retrieval system, without permission in writing from the publishers. No reproduction may be made, whether by photocopying or by any other means, unless a licence has been obtained from the publisher.

Editor: Emma Neale
Design/layout: Fiona Moffat
Author photograph: Philip Temple

Printed in China through Asia Pacific Offset Ltd